THE LAST
BOHEMIAN

THE LAST BOHEMIAN

G. L. Stampa of *Punch*

Edited and Introduced by
Flavia Stampa Gruss

Flavia Stampa Gruss.

BELLEW PUBLISHING

London

OTHER TITLES IN THE CARTOON LIBRARY
(General Editor: Mark Bryant)

Jon's Complete Two Types edited and introduced by Jon
(Foreword by Lord Cudlipp)

The Complete Colonel Blimp edited by Mark Bryant
(Foreword by Rt Hon. Michael Foot, Introduction by Colin Seymour-Ure)

Gibbard's Double Decade Omnibus
edited and introduced by Les Gibbard
(Foreword by John Cole)

First published in Great Britain in 1991 by
Bellew Publishing Company Limited
7 Southampton Place, London WC1A 2DR

ISBN 0 947792 78 3

Printed and bound in Great Britain by Billing & Sons

PREFACE

THIS book has been produced to mark the fortieth anniversary of the death of the celebrated cartoonist and illustrator G. L. Stampa (1875–1951). As far as possible, the illustrations have been reproduced from Stampa's original drawings and this is the first collection of his work to appear since 1948. Publication also coincides with the launch of a special anniversary exhibition of Stampa's art – including many of the cartoons in this book – which has been arranged to tour Britain in 1991/2.

The publishers and the Stampa family would like to thank *Punch* for permission to reproduce these cartoons and in particular David Thomas and Amanda-Jane Doran for their help. I would also like to thank Anthony Verrier, Ib Bellew, Bob Vickers, Mel Calman, Liz Ottaway and especially Mark Bryant who has been consistently encouraging and helpful and without whom this book would not have been.

F. S. G.

The publisher thanks the proprietors of *Punch*
for their special permission to reproduce the drawings
in this book

FOREWORD

David Thomas, Editor of Punch

A FEW years ago, when I first arrived at *Punch*, I was unwise enough to hold a special dinner for all the magazine's cartoonists. Now, cartoonists are, by and large, a strange and unstable breed. Taken individually, they are tough enough to deal with, but en masse they can be a truly terrifying proposition.

Before the meal, I attempted to give a short speech, outlining my editorial policy cartoon-wise. Foolishly, I revealed my feelings about the (then) current state of cartooning in *Punch*, which was that whilst the jokes were still as good as ever, the artists seemed to have lost the knack of capturing the look of the times in their work. Most of the inhabitants of the magazine's drawings seemed to live in a strange Cartoonland, trapped in a mid-Sixties hell of G-plan furniture, pipe-smoking husbands, shapeless wives and non-specific dollybirds.

What a contrast this was, I said, to the *Punch* of days gone by, whose bound volumes captured the look of their respective periods as effectively as any history book. So, I concluded, what I was looking for was a coterie of cartoonists who would draw in such a way that, years from now, people would look at their work and say, 'Yes! that's exactly what the 1990s looked like!'

At this point I was interrupted by a very distinguished, not to say famous, cartoonist. In a broad Lancastrian accent he announced, 'This yoong man knows nothing about comedy. I cannot understand a single word he is saying.' Whereupon he stalked out, never to reappear in *Punch* again.

Now, the reason that I tell this apparently irrelevant tale is that G. L. Stampa's work was a perfect example of the quality I was trying to describe. I have in front of me as I write these words a volume called *Humours of the Street*, a collection of Stampa's *Punch* cartoons published in 1921. In his Introduction to that particular book the humorist W. Pett Ridge wrote:

> Stampa gives himself the trouble of arriving at exactitudes . . . he can take ordinary people and make them interesting. His types are ever exact and true . . . [For example] Stampa knows the youngsters of London. He knows the caps they wear, the boots they put on, the jackets they take off; he can guess with unerring accuracy the words they can use at any crisis.

He might have added that Stampa knew plenty of other people too: the grandes dames of the Edwardian years, the flappers of the Twenties and the theatrical stars of the Thirties, for example. And, as with all the great *Punch* cartoonists, his best jokes are as funny today as they were when first conceived.

I am looking at one now: a beauty, draped in a few minimal whisps of chiffon, is arriving at a ball. A middle-aged couple are watching her with bafflement, mixed with disapproval. 'I'm told she's always writing to her dressmaker about new frocks,' says one of the pair. 'I suppose,' replies the other, 'she enclosed a stamped and addressed envelope for that one.' The drawing could only date from 1921. The joke works just as well in 1991. And that, I suggest, is the mark of Stampa's greatness.

'I'm told she's always writing to her dressmaker about new frocks.'
'I suppose she enclosed a stamped and addressed envelope for that one.'

INTRODUCTION

by Flavia Stampa Gruss

In the earlier years of this century, when photography, radio and television were in their infancy, cartoonists – often undervalued as artists – played an important role in commenting on daily events. George Loraine Stampa's sensitive drawings, executed with care and fidelity, have left us with a delightful and humorous record of these times. Although an acute observer, his wit is kind and gentle, and we are able to follow the touching and funny side of life during one of the most rapidly changing periods of British history – from the hansom cab to the jet. Stampa's unforced humour is the result of personal, sympathetic, observation and study. His mischievous ragamuffins made him famous, but he was equally well known as an illustrator of books and a designer of book-jackets.

THE STAMPA FAMILY

A brief glimpse at George Stampa's background and antecedents gives us some insight into the man and his inherited talent. During the eighth century, Charlemagne had made the French-Italian noble Carlo Lanfranco D'Estampes, then *seigneur* of the towns of Dreux and Etampes near Paris, Governor of Milan and ordered him to fight for the Holy Roman Empire's hold over troublesome Lombardy. From Milan Lanfranco was to found the Italian family, subsequently renamed Stampa, which was, over the centuries, to produce great men of the Church and state and others who would, in due course, travel across the expanding Byzantine Empire. Indeed the Aegean island of Stampalia (renamed Astipalaea after the Second World War), was colonized by the family in the fourteenth century, and after a turbulent Turkish-Greek history, is today inhabited by a peaceful fishing community, its ruined, fortified castle looking out over the dark sea towards the Turkish coast.

Gaspara Stampa, who was born in Padua, in 1520, was, with Vittoria Colonna, perhaps one of the finest poets of the Italian Renaissance and her death by poison in 1554 was the tragic finale to her consuming passion for the Duke of Colalto – immortalized by Titian – whom she had met at a masked ball in Venice. Two years after their meeting he had forsaken her to go and fight in the wars of Henry II of France, thence to fall under the spell of Diane de Poitiers. The exotic strain in the family history is also reflected in volumes of poetry by Ercole and Hermes

9

Stampa. Their work, spanning the seventeenth and eighteenth centuries, may be found in the British Library, although the archive's only copy of Petrus Stampa's treatise on the art of black magic and the occult appears to have been stolen nearly a century ago. On looking through the family's chronicles, one feels that tales about another member of the clan, 'Il Tempo' Stampa, having reached the age of 300 must be exaggerated!

G. L. Stampa's father, Giorgio Domenico, was born in Constantinople in 1835, but was sent to school in England, at Long Marton in Westmorland (now Cumbria) and later articled to the architect Edward Walters of Manchester. Domenico was subsequently responsible for the design of the Manchester Free Trade Hall, and produced a fine watercolour of the building in 1855. In 1872, he married Ann Heelis, the daughter of the Rector of Long Marton, and in 1895 returned with her to live in Constantinople's Italian community. There he became architect to Sultan Abdul Hamid of Turkey, known to the infidel (and, no doubt for good reason, to many of his own subjects) as 'Abdul the Damned'. The British Embassy at Therapia, the Sultan's palace in Constantinople, the palace of the Khedive of Egypt and numerous mosques all bear witness to the inspiration and design of G. D. Stampa.

The three sons, of whom Giorgio (later to become George) Loraine was the second, were born and spent their early childhood in Constantinople. It would appear from the two family mausoleums constructed in the mid-nineteenth century that the Stampas had every intention of remaining there. Indeed, had it not been for the uprisings against the Sultan, which ultimately forced the family to leave Turkey and settle in Ann Stampa's former family home at Battlebarrow House in Appleby near Long Marton in 1878, the Stampa connection with Constantinople might well have lasted into the present time. In 1889, G. D. Stampa had become a naturalized British subject, as had his sons. In their turn this new generation was to be British by adoption, English by education and, for the first time, permanently resident in the country. That Domenico disliked the climate, with its cold winds and draughts, was evident to their more stoic neighbours, and 'Il Conte' must have appeared a rather curious Eastern character as he sat inside a specially made four-sided glass screen from where he could see, hear and join in the conversation without the chilly discomforts of an old country house. Seated thus, he would often smoke his Turkish hookah while keeping his head warm under a fez.

Domenico's eldest son, Lelio, became a history don at Oxford, tutoring among others T. E. Lawrence, who contributed to the Stampa collection of armour when he returned from his Arabian travels by giving him a Crusader's suit of chain-mail. Lelio's early drawings show that he was almost as gifted an artist as his brother George. The youngest of the three brothers, Arturo, was to die of pneumonia at the age of eighteen in 1892.

So it was from ancestors such as these that George inherited his temperament and ability to portray with such accuracy a record of the changing world about him. He grew up in a cosmopolitan family, who confusingly spoke Italian, French, Turkish or English around the dining-table, and where it was simple politeness to reply in whichever language you had been addressed.

EARLY DAYS

G. L. Stampa's childhood sketchbooks show the work of a gifted artist. The proportion and feeling for his subjects is surprisingly mature. Much of his youth was spent in Westmorland, where his first school essays must have afforded his parents some amusement, but show his love for the Cumbrian countryside; 'In spring, primroses and violets bud forth and adorn the gardens with splendour, and the young maidens go rambling to the meadows, watching the gambols of the lately-born lambs.'

In later life, his letters refer to return visits not only with great affection, but with the eye of an artist: 'It was a glorious drive over the fells, the effect of sky and hills very beautiful in their changes. It turned to rain when we came back, which gave an effect beyond the skill of any painter – I should say *artist* because

 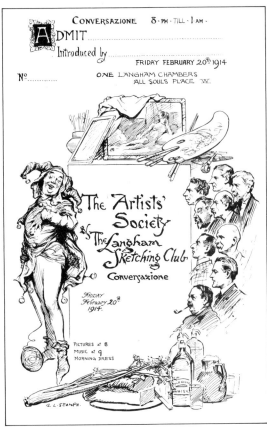

Left: A typical sketch made by Stampa at the Langham Sketching Club, London. The original measures 327mm x 146mm.
Right: Design by Stampa for an invitation for a *conversazione* evening of the Artists' Society and the Langham Sketching Club on 20 February 1914, drawn in ink on O.W. Ordinary Pasteboard.

I often think there are more painters than artists in the world, and the two are not always connected.' A keen fisherman, the young Stampa spent much of his spare time in Appleby on the riverbank with one of his favourite cousins, Willy Heelis (later to marry Beatrix Potter): 'The clouds were lying low on the fells and there was a real Westmorland downpour. Willy and I have had a week of fairish sport – his catch was fifty-two, in spite of the weather.'

Leaving Appleby Grammar when he was eleven years old, George was then enrolled at Bedford Modern School near London from where he went on to study painting and drawing at Heatherley's School of Art in 1892. After three years at Heatherley's he won a five-year scholarship to the Royal Academy Schools, and from that time on London was to become his home. Here he lived at 22 Comeragh Rd, West Kensington, and shared a studio in Abbey Road, St John's Wood, with another artist, Savile Lumley (later to achieve fame with 'Daddy, What Did You Do in the Great War?'). Fellow students at the RA included W. Heath Robinson and Lewis Baumer amongst others. He graduated in 1900 and, having been a regular contributor to *Punch* since the age of nineteen, now became a full-time illustrator and cartoonist, working mainly for *Punch* but also contributing to the *Bystander, Humorist, Graphic, Strand Magazine* etc. He also began to spend many afternoons at the Langham Sketching Club in All Souls Place near Regent Street where artists would gather informally to draw nudes from life. To capture the movements of animals Stampa became a Life Member of the London Zoo.

When G. L. S., as he became known, married Ethel Crowther in 1906, they made the Hampstead area their home, and it was there that their only son, Arthur, was born in 1908. By all accounts the Stampas' domestic life appears to have been happy. Ethel's sister Eleanor Crowther moved in with the couple soon after their marriage and the somewhat eccentric 'Aunt Eleanor' – in contrast to the self-effacing, rather saintly Mrs Stampa – would remain a constant household companion of the family until his death.

Deemed unfit for service at the outbreak of the First World War, Stampa visited Westmorland again in 1917 and spent some time sketching the wounded soldiers in Appleby Hospital, managing to make himself temporarily unpopular by absentmindedly tipping cigarette ash into a nearby upturned ear trumpet! Travelling north he wrote, was a 'welcome respite from very long dark nights with zeppelins. Poor old England – our cricket was a sad affair! I consoled myself by watching the local match yesterday. The Pro who had lost his left hand – bitten off by a motor-mower – was fielding but not batting, very handicapped, of course. Some wickets fell, but the only catch was by an old fisherman sitting on the riverbank.'

STAMPA AND *PUNCH*

G. L. S's first *Punch* drawing 'The Decoration', appeared in March 1894, when the magazine was edited by Francis Burnand. He had encouraged the young artist while he was still a student at Heatherley's, and a collection of Burnand's large and almost illegibly scrawled letters in the possession of the family

Is it worth while, Mr Hochstetter?
Fancy portrait of Mr Hochstetter composing 'The German Greeting' and of an average
Englishman trembling as he reads the translation in his morning paper.

'. . . meanwhile in Britain, the entire population, faced by the threat of invasion, has been flung
into a state of complete panic.'

Stampa's dynamic drawing of February 1915 finds echoes in the Second World War in
Pont's well known *Punch* cartoon of 14 August 1940. (*Lüstige Blätter* was one of the
leading German satirical journals.)

show the friendship that developed between G. L. S. and his mentor. Stampa was greatly influenced by his predecessors on *Punch* – in particular Charles Keene, remembered for his portraits of working-class Victorians, and Phil May, with his drawings of urchins and cockneys – and his early work has some similarity to theirs, with much close-lined shading and rather studied Victorian attitudes.

Stampa, however, soon developed his own distinct contribution to *Punch*: a tolerant, not merely a humorous view of the world. *Punch* was launched in 1841 as a magazine with decidedly political leanings, likely to poke sharp fun at Conservative and Liberal parties alike, and Keene and May indirectly reflected this stance. However, by the time that G. L. S. began to draw for Burnand, the magazine had become one of gently ironic social comment and the young artist was very much at home in such an atmosphere. Indeed, in the course of his long association with *Punch*, he did much to foster it.

A typical example of Stampa's 'At the Play' illustration for the theatre pages of *Punch*. This one was published in 1936 and depicts a scene from 'A Dressing-room Interlude' at the Phoenix Theatre starring Noel Coward, Alan Webb and Gertrude Lawrence.

G.L.S. drew the first-night theatre cartoons, 'At the Play', for *Punch* throughout much of his career, signing some of his work 'Harris Brooks', and was succeeded by Ronald Searle. A working artist, he would sometimes go to first nights two or three times a week, returning to his studio to finish his drawings for the *Punch* deadline. Theatre nights, week after week, were not always easy for him, as the following extract from a letter to his son shows.

The first night of the 'Golden Eagle' at the Westminster was well dressed and acted, but I felt it rather long drawn out and, from my point of view, very difficult to see what I was doing and, therefore, unsatisfactory and disappointing . . . My last few theatres have been very boring. I think the production must have been at fault, as I remember enjoying 'Quality Street' the first time I saw it. The next was 'Emma' from Jane Austen's book, but it doesn't make a play.

However, one or two theatre sketches show him seated comfortably with a colleague at a table with glasses and wine, so one can presume that he found some evenings bearable. A Christmas card from Gertrude Lawrence is among a collection of those from many actors and actresses who expressed pleasure at his faithfully executed and never cruel impressions of them.

Although 'the sin of procrastination has been mine through life', between 1894 and his last submission – 'Impression for Parliament' – in 1949, G. L. S. managed to contribute 2,500 drawings to *Punch* alone. On one occasion, in 1916, the Art Editor heard a good joke, which he sent to Stampa to illustrate. Back came a note, which read 'many thanks for the jest, but Keene did the same thing so well so long ago, that I'd rather leave it, if you don't mind. G. L. S.' This note expresses Stampa's invariable modesty and sense of proportion. These characteristics should never be forgotten, because he was known to be one of the most brilliant and entertaining of the school of 'character' artists, and was well loved at *Punch*. Alan Agnew, the paper's proprietor, was to write, on his death in 1951, of Stampa's 'irrepressible cheerfulness and kindness'.

OTHER WORK

G. L. S. often gave his drawings to charitable causes, and contributed to a number of 'souvenir' books and benefit programmes including *In a Good Cause* (1900) for the Great Ormond Street Children's Hospital, and the *Literary Pageant* in aid of the Middlesex Hospital. He also contributed to a souvenir theatre programme for sufferers from the *Liberté* disaster (an explosion in Toulon) and 'An admirable Souvenir, with one outstanding dramatic picture by G. L. Stampa' was devised for a benefit matinée at the Hippodrome in London. G. L. S. even once agreed to appear onstage as a 'waiter in a coffee house' in a charity performance produced at Devonshire House and described in the press under the headline: 'Famous People in Bulwer Lytton Play'. (However, the only theatre scenery G. L. S. painted was a 'gallery of ancestors' for a play by 'Hanky Panky John' Macdonald Hastings, put on in Manchester.) In 1925, he contributed a drawing for a performance at the Lyceum Theatre, in aid of the Newspaper Press Fund charities; in September 1928 he gave a painting for the programme for the tribute to Basil Macdonald Hastings, which was afterwards auctioned; and in November 1937 he drew for the Rudyard Kipling Memorial Fund. A letter from Queen Mary also shows how delighted she was with a postage-stamp-size cartoon (the only one commissioned) that G. L. S. drew especially for her prestigious Doll's House.

Stampa was always in demand to design and draw Christmas cards for clubs and societies including, in 1916, a card for the British Expeditionary Force. It was produced for the 19th (Western) Division, and a member wrote, 'It is so exactly what we wanted we feel that you are entitled to a warm vote of thanks.' He also illustrated several books by E. V. Lucas and of one *The Times* in 1922 reported, 'Mr. Stampa makes the perfect illustrator for Mr. Lucas. He does not always cling to the letter; he likes to play round it, embellish it, enrich it, always maintaining agreement between his own humour and the humour of the author. This is the right way of illustrating.' In addition, he illustrated books by A. P. Herbert, Anthony Armstrong and Rudyard Kipling.

Illustration from 'Toby Dog' in Kipling's *Thy Servant a Dog* (1930). Captioned in the
book as 'I called', Stampa's own caption was 'Boots gives tongue till daylight'.
The Black Aberdeen, Boots, who tells the story about his adventures with his friend
Ravager, was in fact Stampa's own dog.

G. L. S.'s first Kipling illustration was in 1928, for 'The Black Aberdeen'
in the *Strand Magazine*; the book *Thy Servant a Dog* followed in 1930. The
Kipling archives at Sussex University reveal that Mrs Kipling's reaction to his
drawings were very favourable, especially as his drawings of animals were never
'saccharine', and she wrote to her husband's agent, A. P. Watt, 'We are so glad
that Mr Stampa is going ahead . . .' and later that, 'The illustrations have given
Mr Kipling much pleasure . . . the style is admirably suited to his subject matter.'
Mrs Kipling was known as a woman not only much given to interference, but
also as one who was excessively hard to please. Praise from her was praise indeed.
Stampa also published four volumes on his own work: *Loud Laughter* (1907)
Ragamuffins (1916), *Humours of the Street* (1921) and *In Praise of Dogs* (1948).

Covers of three of Stampa's collections.

Of *Ragamuffins* one critic wrote: 'The unwashed adult had for long been known as a creature of wit, mirth, tragedy and philosophy; and now the unwashed child is seen with all these qualities and an added grace.' Children were an important part in Stampa's life. In an interview with the *Daily Chronicle*, published in 1924, Stampa said,

I am never so happy as when I see a crowd of ragamuffins at play, either in the streets or in the parks. You'll see a rowdy game of cricket or football going on, or a young riot, with a mass of small humanity on top of some unlucky little beggar at the bottom, all kicking legs and tousled heads, with probably a dog or two barking round, when suddenly you'll be struck by one thing – the young street Arab's seriousness. He probably hasn't a care in the world, except a carefully nursed revenge for some enemy urchin who blacked his eye last week, yet you'll notice him quietly disentangling himself from the mêlée, and watch his comrades with intent seriousness, just like a sparrow. But they have their sad side too – sometimes you see it in their serious little faces that fill with perplexity at the problems of life, and it's no use, you have to turn away.

In another review in February 1917 the *Daily Chronicle* described him as not only 'a master of black and white . . . but a humorist in the great Leech tradition'. Of *Humours of the Street*, the *Bookman* wrote,

His work is so strongly individual that even those of us who are no expert need no signature to prove his title to it. Stampa knows urchins as a scholar knows his books, his humour is the more telling because of its freedom from exaggeration; he can be funny without giving his characters impossible noses or distorting their faces or figures. There is enough in this book alone to establish him in the front rank of humorous artists and artistic humorists.

John O'London's Weekly added true words of praise, 'What can one say of George Stampa, the kindest-hearted humorist who ever laughed at human folly; of all the succesful men I have ever met in London, he is the most approachable.'

THE GENIAL ECCENTRIC

A quiet, modest man with an impish sense of humour, G. L. S. cared little for his appearance and usually wore what he referred to as his 'winter tweedings', complete with waistcoat, watch-chain and slightly crooked bow-tie. His pockets were weighed down with a sketchbook and a handful of short, stubby pencils – new pencils were immediately cut into four pieces. Thus attired and equipped, G. L. S. would set out on his London perambulations, observing, noting, recording life as it struck him or aroused his concern. His quality as an artist lay in an unusual blend of sympathy and detachment. Sympathy led him to observe and record, while detachment, as a bystander rather than participant, gave him the power to illustrate human (and animal) foibles as they are, not only as his age saw them. The revival of interest in Stampa's art today is not, for these reasons, at all surprising, although it is certainly overdue. But there can be little doubt that he would be mildly amused by the popularity of his work in the 1980s and 1990s.

Stampa's traits were well known and mostly endearing. He smoked incessantly, whether a pipe, a cigar or one of his own rolled cigarettes, and in a letter to his son in 1946 he wrote, 'It is very late, and very shortly I shall have my last but one cigarette, then my absolute final, and then do likewise.' Always compassionate, one of his letters describes the saga of a long telephone conversation with an inpecunious stranger – the acquaintance of a friend – and the subsequent and

G. L. S. working at his easel at 8 The Ridgeway, Golders Green.

inconvenient trip late at night across London to give the man £10. The *Daily Graphic*, in 1926, reported, 'He is the best of good fellows and the kind of Bohemian to whom no stockbroker dare condescend, and though others pose for him, he never poses himself.' *John O'London's Weekly* described him as 'The most cheerful, contented and amiable inhabitant of what is called Bohemian London. He never envies anyone and sincerely appreciates the work of his rivals. The consequence is that no man has a larger number of friends.'

Stampa had certain magpie tendencies. A collector of unconsidered trifles, one is left to wonder what, if anything, he intended to do with the mounds of torn-off calendar stubs and neat little piles of silver paper from cigarette packets. Collecting illustrated and amusing letters from friends is more understandable, and from among many postcards with cryptic messages one, sent in 1937, reads, 'The Duchess is dead, alas! She died before we left Liverpool. The North was apparently too cold for her!'

THE SAVAGE CLUB

As meticulously filled-in score sheets show, the fact that Lord's Cricket Ground was only a few miles from his house was no accident, his leisure time being divided equally between cricket and the Savage Club, to which he was elected in 1911 (one of his sponsors being *Punch*'s Leonard Raven-Hill) and later became one of the Trustees. In 1940, the Stampas' house at 8 The Ridgeway, Golders Green, was bombed in their absence, and for a while they moved south, to Oxshott in Surrey. To a friend, he wrote, 'We have been living here since September, when we were blown out of The Ridgeway, and will I fear, remain for some time. Doors shattered, windows blown out, ceiling blown down and tiles blown off. "Blow, blow, thou winter wind!" Hardly relevant, but I feel I have to round off a sentence when addressing an esteemed colleague with literary tastes.'

Savage Club menu for a dinner on 21 January 1928 chaired by A. P. Herbert. The meal consisted of mulligatawny soup, roast ribs of beef with vegetables, rhubarb pie and cream, soft roes on toast, and coffee.

As a member of the Savage Club, which was, at that time, a genuinely Bohemian tribe of artists and literary men, G. L. S. regularly attended the monthly dinners, for which he produced the majority of the Club's amusingly illustrated menus. He always took the Chair at Christmas, in the company of such friends as J. M. Barrie, E. H. Shepard, Benno Moiseiwitch and A. P. Herbert. The artists drew sketches of one another on the back of place cards, or at the top of lengthy and appetizing menus that invariably read something like:'Caviar and *blinis, Tortue claire, Turbotin dorine, Perdreau roti, Omelette surprise* and *Os à la moëlle.*'

One evening ended with G. L. S., Alfred Munnings and a third reveller tumbling down the London Underground escalator into a heap at the bottom, and ignominiously being picked up by helpful passers-by. A. P. Herbert was a particular friend, of whom he drew many caricatures. For a bet, he wrote G. L. S. a cheque on a Savage Club napkin; and Stampa repaid by writing his on the back of a borrowed pig – both were cashed! George Baker, an eminent singer of the time, wrote, 'The Savage Club always had the cream of the black-and-white artists of note . . . that splendid old fellow George Stampa.' C. E. Lawrence, the Honorary Secretary, wrote to him in 1925, 'Because you are you, the best of splendiferous fellows, and a great Savage, your Jubilee is to be celebrated on November 29th . . .'

THE ARTIST AFLOAT

Many of Stampa's sketches were made during the cruises he took in the 1920s and 1930s with Lawrence Bradbury – a member of the third generation of *Punch* owners, and some thirteen years his senior – to the Far East, South Africa, South America and the Baltic.

Stampa had always suffered in the cold weather and, after rheumatic fever in 1926, tried to take voyages to sunnier climes during the winter. A press-cutting of the period reads: 'Mr. G. L. Stampa, artist, a famous Bohemian, sails today for a three-month cruise of the African coast. Stampa has, for over twenty years, been one of the main supports of *Punch*, and his dog pictures have no equal.' A month later, G. L. S. wrote home to his wife, 'Poor Bradbury complains that the Marconi man [the wireless operator] plays his gramophone with a very loud needle and very American jazz records . . . It is much too hot and wet to sketch, and I sit on deck getting as much breeze as possible, and watching flying fish "playing" as Kippers [Kipling] puts it.' After he had left South Africa, a friend in Beira wrote to him: 'The portrait you executed so faithfully in Worcestershire Sauce, of our friend Lawley of the Savoy Hotel (which the Rhodesian Railways has bought lock, stock and barrel), has been entirely eaten by cockroaches.'

From the Far East, his son received a card, 'In Batavia, the rickshaw boys pestered to take us "plenty long way" for a moderate fee and, as Bradbury's "Go to hell!" had no effect, we ended up by being trotted over the Chinese quarter – two sweating bodies, and mine had a moth-eaten head. I liked it, though very smelly – the streets, I mean, not the head.' In 1927, Bradbury and G. L. S. crossed the Equator in the SS *Highland Rover*, and he wrote that, 'The Captain is

Cruising on the SS *J. P. Coen*, 29 January to 5 March 1931. Stampa often went on cruises when he had recurrences of rheumatic fever. On the back of this photo Captain Ferwiel has written under the caption 'The Dice Club': 'You can't choose your family, but you can pick out your friends. I hope you will count me one of them.' John J. Plieger (presumably the man on Stampa's left) has added 'So say I' and the last shakily written signature is that of the fourth member of the party, W. L. Bradbury of *Punch*.

a good sort, with a merry eye, dressed in a coat buttoned up to the neck, who holds himself as straight as a gentleman. He had to let the ship down a bit because of fearsome high seas and strong winds, which made my shave and bath an acrobatic feat.' Some of his studies of animals were also drawn on board. 'We have some prize sheep, cocks and hens being sent out to the Argentine. None has much space at their disposal, and I visit them now and again to give them a few words of comfort.' At the end of their trip to South America, he sent home another letter in the usual neat, tiny writing. 'I am glad to be back on board. Our Hotel Paris in Rio Grande was alive with beetles, flies and ants and I am very bitten.'

While cruising, G. L. S. often made use of a camera to record occasions that he did not have time to draw. 'There is such a rush on shore that I have insufficient time for sketching, and I depend a lot on the Box Brownie Arthur gave me, but it plays tricks and I have fears that it will let me down.' The voyages also provided G. L. S. with new colours: 'Magnificent sunsets and sunrises that I have seen nothing to equal, such a depth of colour that the sunsets beat all my powers of description. The sea is a rich clear blue, and the sky not so cloudy as it has been.'

These words provide a clue to the many threads in George Stampa's background character, temperament and art. He was a man who cared deeply for England and things English. Although given to nostalgia, G. L. S. was at home in the world of his life and times which, however Bohemian (of the gentler sort), remained one of 'an English sun under an English Heaven'. Yet we should never forget that G. L. S. gained from his Italian forebears a special warmth and lightness of touch – the ragamuffins of Seven Dials were the blood brothers of those of Venice and Milan.

He was very much a man of his times, an honoured member of a family of ancient descent. Perhaps Hilaire Belloc's words best form an epitaph:

> From quiet homes and first beginning,
>   Out to the undiscovered ends,
> There's nothing worth the wear of winning,
>   But laughter and the love of friends.

THE LAST
BOHEMIAN

Jobbing Gardener: 'This garden's overrun with slugs, sir. I can't keep pace with 'em.'
Owner: 'Yes, I've noticed them whizzing by you.'

'Be a good boy and stop your 'ollerin' – and I'll let you see the old gent
fall off the bus!'

'This damp weather brings out your rheumatism, eh?'
'*Who*'s got rheumatism? Damme, this is my football knee!'

'He's eaten it!'

Agent: 'Can I interest you in a vacuum-cleaner?
Maid: 'Not 'ere, sir. We don't keep vacuums.'

'Have you given the goldfish their fresh water today?'
'No, ma'am, they haven't drunk up what I gave 'em yesterday.'

'Would any of you gentlemen like a game of poker?'

Observant Lady (to gentleman alighting from bus):
'I think you've dropped a penny.'

1st Doctor (referring to millionaire patient): 'He will recover.'
2nd Doctor: 'I think so too. We have got over the worst.'
1st Doctor: 'No. The worst is yet to come. We have to inform the relatives.'

Mr L. Forleather (taking his friend the landscape painter to see the country):
'Tell me when you're stuck on any particular view.'

'Lumme – readin' again, always *readin'*! Ain't yer got a mind of yer own?'

'I have just had the house redecorated throughout. It is ready for immediate occupation, unless of course your ideas of decoration are very fantastic.'

Boarding the last bus after a great Pacifist rally.

31

'Quick! Come and tell Granny what's wrong with her motorbike!'

Bobbie (to Auntie blowing bubbles to amuse him):
'Fed up with balloons – blow an aeroplane!'

'Do you wish me to summon Berlin or Rome, Your Grace?'

Strategy
Since little Binley hit on the device of carrying two empty boxes, well labelled,
motorists treat him with respect and he crosses the road anywhere in safety.

Hired Butler (announcing guest at fancy-dress ball):
'Time, gentlemen, please!'

Marjorie (in smoking carriage): 'Won't the guard be very cross, Mummy, if we don't smoke?'

Boarding-house Landlady: 'Take your pick, Mr Summers.'
Second Lodger: 'You'll need it, old man.'

Wife: 'I think you're a pig – you never agree to anything I suggest!'
Husband: 'All right, old thing; do it if you're so keen on it. I'd like you to.'
Wife: 'I'll do nothing of the kind – why should you always have your own way.'

Real Artist: 'Were they all artistic people you met there?'
She: 'Some of them were, but some were quite nice.'

American: 'These guys, Junior,
are the Horse Guards.'
Junior: 'What's the big idea, Pop?
That horse don't look as if he
needs guarding!'

'How can you say I've got the
better of the bargain when you
haven't seen the car I've got?'
'I saw the car you had.'

Remarks that don't ring true
Distinguished Specialist: 'Have this prescription made up or – er – not, just as you feel inclined. It will make no difference!'

'I can't speak too highly of today's Special, sir. It's all we've got left.'

'I suppose now that you boys are mechanized, the distance to Tipperary
is nothing to make a noise about.'

Chatterbox Wife (entertaining talkative friend in author's study): 'Go on with your
writing, dear. Muriel will excuse you.'

Wife: Lumme! To git anythink aht o' you's like tryin' to open an oyster
with a bus ticket!'

Charlady (who has dusted pastel drawing in studio): Lumme! It's a *movie*!'

Lady (to famous novelist): 'I've been buying a number of your books
for the long dreary evenings.'

Customer: 'What in the world's "Bungalow Fluff"?'
Waitress: 'Well, it was "Cottage Pudding" yesterday,
but it didn't go very well.'

Owner of Alsatian: 'Throw your arms around her – stop her. I lost her for a week and now she's running wild!'

Very Modern (showing friend over new house):
'I'm thinking out a design to paint on this window.
The view is so hideously Victorian.'

Perfect Shopman (to customer who has been overwhelmed in fierce charge of bargain-hunters): 'Are you being attended to, moddom?'

Film Star: 'I love you, darling, in my own inimitable way.'

'May I say yer out?'

Little Girl (entering carriage with her mother and being glowered at by occupants):
'Mummy, next stop it'll be *our* turn to hate!'

'Take a – er – a sofa, old man.'

Young Wife (at sound of explosion): 'Thomas! Thomas! The Zeppelins are here!
Did you lock the front door?'

Trifling

He: 'I love you with all my *heart,* with all my *mind*, my every *thought*, my –
She (interrupting): 'Yes, I know. But all that means so little!'

'That's the second time this term, Hawkins Minor, that you've asked me whether Himmler was once a schoolmaster.'

'What I need is activity. Damme, when I am at war I *am* at war!'

'We fell out, my wife and I'

He: 'That's absurd! Do you think I'm as big a fool as I look?'

She: 'I think that if you aren't, you have a great deal to be thankful for!'

Loafer: 'Would you kindly gimme a subscription, madam, for a Society
as I belongs to?'
Lady: 'What's the Society?'
Loafer: 'It's – er – well, it's a *Public* Society. We enters 'ouses, madam,
for the purpose o' puttin' down the Drink.'

51

Neglected Diner (to waiter): 'I finished the menu long ago.
I'm rather a quick reader.'

'Positively nothing exactly what I want. Most customers would be annoyed
but I can see the funny side of it.'

'Cousin Agatha doesn't know the way from the station, dear, so ring them again
and ask if the 11.45 is nearly due yet.'

Exclusive Person (entering dining-room of his club): 'Dammit!
Where the doose can I go? There's somebody got my table!'

'Are you seeking Yuletide Gifts or merely Christmas presents, madam?'

Art for Art's Sake

Our painter poets always show inspiration coming to them something like this –

But they always leave out the inspiring bit.

Little Man: 'Wot's your 'obby when you're at 'ome like?'
The Other: 'Keepin' love-birds.'

'One day I were surrounded by a dozen of 'em. Like giants they was and savage as lions
– any one of 'em could a' swung me round 'is 'ead with one 'and!'
'Lor! An 'ow did yer get away?'
'Killed 'em.'

She: ' Is insanity a cause for divorce?'
He: 'No – it's the cause of marriage!'

Professor of Music (to man at piano who is burlesquing a classic):
'You were given a funny face, boy – be satisfied with that.'

Scene – Express train, two hours before the first stop
Stranger: 'In that parcel, sir, under your seat, I have the greatest invention of the age.
It contains the most deadly and powerful explosive ever discovered. I'm going to patent it
today if it doesn't go off accidently before I get to London.'
Nervous Gentleman: 'B-but s-supposing-it-does-go off-in *here*-w-what then?'
Stranger: 'Then, sir, it doesn't matter; the secret dies with me.'

'You shouldn't take any notice of the parrot, Mary. Why, he's old enough to be your grandfather!'

'William, take the lady to the Bargain Basement!'

Wife: 'Are you wet, dear?'
Husband: 'No, darling, but my feet are a bit sunburnt.'

Side show at travelling circus
Showman: 'Ladies and Gents, I 'ave to ask your indulgence for a few minutes' delay in presentin' the Performin' Fleas owing to a technical 'itch.'

Collector: 'What's this, sir? Your ticket's for St Albans and the train's going to Oxford.'
Passenger (after a long and merry evening): 'Well don't stand there arguing about it
– go an' tell the driver!'

The Vicar (to parishioner who has violent quarrels with her neighbour): 'Mrs Gabbe sent
a message that she has quite forgiven you. What message can I take to her?'
Parishioner: You can say I 'ope she'll die 'appy.'

'I'll pay you £3 a week starting now – in three months I'll raise it to £3.10.'
'Righto! I'll look in again in three months.'

Remarks that don't ring true
Painter of the Old School: 'Their colour may not be so vivid, perhaps
– but these Moderns *draw* so much better than we do.'

'What exactly is *entrecôte de boeuf marché noir*?

The loser's revenge.

'Doesn't it make me look ridiculous?'
'Very fashionable, modom. If you don't *look* ridiculous
you *are* ridiculous.'

'Yours was the little sailor hat, wasn't it?'

There were embarrassing moments while staying at Moated Grange after the alterations.
It was a mistake converting Sir Murgatroyd's private den into a bathroom.

Remarks that don't ring true
Struggling Artist (to very rich person): 'I cannot accept the commission to paint your
wife's portrait for a thousand pounds – I couldn't hope to do her justice.'

'Waste of a good chair, I call it. Nobody's ever sat on it!'

Nervous Servant (to noble duke): Grace, Your Grouse?'

Burglar (who has made an easy haul, to householder): 'You don't often get burglars 'ere, sir, from the look of it.'

Feminine Amenities
'*Do* take my seat. You're ever so much older than I am.'

'Just clean the inside of the window, Mary, so that I can see out, but leave the outside so that the Smiths can't see in.'

Illusionist's Wife (on arrival at holiday destination): 'Just the sort of thing you would do! Packed everything in the disappearing trunk!'

'Have you got anything sinister?'

'D-don't shout so – *I*'m not deaf.'
'But *I* like to hear what I'm saying.'

BIBLIOGRAPHY

Publications

Loud Laughter, humorous drawings in colour illustrating *Easy French Exercises* (London, Cassell, 1907)

Ragamuffins, a collection of character drawings from *Punch* of street urchins. Sixty-five drawings by G. L. Stampa with an introductory note by A. E. Johnson (London, Duckworth, 1916)

Humours of the Street, drawings of life and character, with an introduction by W. Pett Ridge (London, Methuen, 1921)

In Praise of Dogs, an anthology compiled and illustrated by G. L. Stampa (London, Frederick Muller, 1948)

Book Illustrations

Bertram Atkey, *Easy Money*, the genuine book of Henry Mitch, his diligent search for other folk's wealth, and his urgent fear of the feminine (London, Grant Richards, 1908)

Anthony Armstrong, *Easy Warriors* (London, Methuen, 1923)

Stevenson Lyle Cummins, *Plays for Children* (London, Methuen, 1922)

B. M. Hastings, *Memoirs of a Child* (London, A. N. M. Philpot, 1926)

A. P. Herbert, *Ballads for Broadbows* (London, Ernest Benn, 1930)

Rudyard Kipling, *Supplications of the Black Aberdeen* (New York and London, Doubleday, 1929)

    Thy Servant a Dog told by Boots, edited by Rudyard Kipling (London, Macmillan, 1930)

    Collected Dog Stories (London, Macmillan, 1934)

E. V. Lucas, *Specially Selected:* a choice of essays, with a pictorial commentary (London, Methuen, 1920)

    Urbanites: essays new and old, with a pictorial commentary (London, Methuen, 1921)

A. Maitland Murray *Georgie M'culloch* (London, John Lane/The Bodley Head, 1933)

Joe Walker, *My Dog and Yours* (London and Melbourne, Ward Lock, 1929)

    That Dog of Mine (London and Melbourne, Ward Lock, 1930)

    Two Donkeys for a Week that is to say seven stories about Blanco and Negro written not by, but for, John Stephen (Oxford University Press, 1930)

Magazine Contributions

The Bystander

Cassell's Magazine

The Graphic (1910)

The Homeland Annual

The Humorist

In a Good Cause – Mr Punch's Souvenir (1900) in aid of Mr Punch's Fund for the Hospital for Sick Children, Great Ormond Street

London Opinion

Moonshine (1898)

The Odd Volume (1915)

The Pall Mall Magazine

Printer's Pie (1909 and 1917)

Punch (1895–1951)

The Sketch

The Strand Magazine

The Tatler

Toc H Annual

TP's Magazine (April 1911)

The Windsor Magazine

Winter's Pie (1912)